I0187303

LUMMOX PRESS

WHOSE CRIES ARE NOT MUSIC

By LINDA BENNINGHOFF

ISBN 978-1-929878-95-6

First edition

Lummox Press
PO Box 5301
San Pedro, CA 90733
www.lummoxpress.com

Printed in the United States of America

Cover painting by Barbara Jo Kingsley

Acknowledgments

These poems were published in the following chapbooks:

Parts of section one in Snowy Winter, (published by Pudding House Press); parts of section two in The Street Where I Was a Child (Finishing Line Press); parts of section four in Departures (March Street Press) and The Spaces Between Things (Erbacce Press); section five in Remembering the Catbird (Mipoesias online).

These poems or versions of these poems were also published in the following magazines or anthologies:

Canada Geese: *Poetry Super Highway* (where it won a contest), *Erbacce, Stirring, Poetry Depth, Quarterly;* **This Silence:** *Poetry Billboard;* **After Five Years:** *The Peoples Poet Anthology, The Journal, i-outlaw*, an audio presentation online; **Four Deer:** *MiPoesias;* **Going for Chemo:** *Ocho;* **Reply to Rilke:** *Ocho;* **Under a Morning That Has No Blossoms:** *The Journal, Long Island Sounds Anthology;* **Gulls:** *Canary: a Journal of the Environmental Crisis;* **Whose Cries Are Not Music:** *Youtube*, a short film made by Belinda Subramon. *Pegasus;* **The Moose:** *For Poets Only;* **After Leaving, Evening With My Father, The Street Where I Was a Child,** and **August:** *Hidden Oak;* **The Summer House:** *The Journal;* **This Cat:** *Creature Features* (an animal magazine).

WHOSE
CRIES
ARE NOT
MUSIC

TABLE OF CONTENTS

INTRODUCTION

I RUMMAGE THROUGH A LOT OF POETS these days. Anyone can, despite the clutter and confusion. I believe we live in a time when there is an embarrassment of wealth in poetic talent. What are we to do with it? For me, it seems to winnow out into poems that are ineffective for one reason or other, poems that rock me, and poems that I can learn from. The poetry of Linda Benninghoff is very rare to me, in that it lives in the second and third categories at the same time. My first comment on the collection "Departures" was that I "take instruction" from it. I resonate with it, and I see the talent that speaks so clearly and simply that I can watch the workings of it all. This volume contains "Departures" and much more. It is your opportunity to catch up on an overlooked gem.

Here is an excerpt from "Snowy Winter"…bear in mind that this fairly short poem has many more interwoven metaphors:

"… The creamy snow extends even to the water,
where there are wrinkles and marks
—frozen over
from Lloyd to Cold Spring Harbor.
The curving gulls
keep saying the words you spoke.
Yet there is no food for them here,
they rest in the empty air
hungry like me,

as I search
for the prints of winter birds..."

I see the aging skin and a glossing over at the
exact same time, a duel metaphor with a cruel
dissonance, a sweeping of the cold in a rhetorical
style that reminds me of James Joyce, a haunting
by the gulls, the tie-back to personal emptiness
(note: a second double-metaphor!) which crosses
over into the psychology of sublimation. That's
a first-order reading. There is so much that
telegraphs from this one stanza that I simply
cannot find in entire poems, because their attempts
somehow suffocate on overreaching words or
functionally illogical metaphor. This little passage
shows what you can do with a few carefully chosen
words and structures. It rings to the feeling. It puts
you there.

Lao Tzu said, "Govern a great nation as
you would cook a small fish. Do not overdo
it." As a chef, I've always loved that, and as a
poet, I am always mindful of the edge between
the toasted and the burnt. Each poem is like
a nation, influence spreading far beyond its
words. Evocation is the best measure of it. So
many collections try too hard. This has a more
open-eyed, careful, unforced feeling to it. It is
stunning sometimes how Linda's poems achieve
their flavor without a lot of complicated verbiage
or reference to other works. The way she weaves
landscape, animals, the artifacts of our lives, and
emotions is actually an intricate achievement,
but in the end, there are poems that make the

"I" of the prose a consequence of the world, with
a strange belonging, even in sadness, a reverse
solipsism, as though the world in fact thinks us
up. The similarities to Shamanism are striking.
Linda is direct and earnest with her entrainment
of the natural world to speak for her life. If I can
infuse even part of what I write with this careful
spirituality, I have invested my time well. If
you are just reading this to enjoy as literature, I
think this is a great read. Take your time; like
watching for deer, much hides in the open.

Jim Knowles

I.

DO THE DEAD?

SNOWY WINTER

I remember
the praying silence
of the pots in the kitchen
after I washed them.
In April, when we went jogging
you ordered
mango juice from the new
concession.
"Don't worry about the future,
I can always take care of you," you said.
"I feel so frightened when I am alone."

You live by yourself now
in a house with pale furniture.
I live in a place where
the ice closes in on me
in winters which are like a world shutting down.
My Christmas cards to you show
pictures of reindeer,
children opening packages
under trees,
skaters at Rockefeller Center.
their faces red like apples.

The creamy snow extends even to the water,
where there are wrinkles and marks
—frozen over
from Lloyd to Cold Spring Harbor.
The curving gulls
keep saying the words you spoke,

yet there is no food for them here.
They rest in the empty air
hungry like me,
as I search
for the prints of winter birds.

FOR MOTHER

The purple flowers of the lilac
are in your hand,
I picture you pressing them
into the book you are reading,
the way I see you now
at age 80
your busy face,
hands like iron,
your will that wanted to work good in the world
but could only enclose us
this small house, quiet family.

The lilac scent rages
like ragged angels singing,
like our dog who died at age twelve
barking at two squirrels with twitching tails,
the three playing in undying sun.

Going For Chemo

There was
the silence
of the pots
after they were washed,
put on the rack to dry.

That evening a dead seagull lay
flat like paper on the causeway.

You touched the gray
in your splintery, falling-out hair.
We were going out
getting ice cream.
Back inside
the teapot
made a sound
I remembered
long after that day,
a sound like robins praying.

SNOW

The snow sleeps over the earth.
I am doing laundry—
Mother asks—did you put
your blue pajamas in, the towels?
On snow days at age six
home from school
I would play till my lips froze.
Now the mice are the merriest,
nesting near the warm oil burner
in the basement, drumming
their feet against the ceiling—
a sound like dry sticks twitching.

Reply to Rilke

Not to hear even one's first name mentioned.
This must be death. In the underworld,
I cannot glimpse the spring coming,
smell the fresh-cut grass.
Dandelions don't spot the field.
Who are the angels? Do they come to us
even in death, and slowly lift us
from oblivion?

These flowers shine brightly. They take the stars
away.

I fear the winter but the spring more.
The first crocus bloom is
terrible under the March sun.
I feel the dim shoots of change,
pushing from underneath, the soil
growing moist instead of caked and hard.

DEER

They came to Lloyd Neck seeking
new grass and bushes,
a place to roam unseen.

I saw them running through
our yard,
sometimes just brown
backs catching sunlight.

Yesterday four deer ran through,
two mothers,
two fawns,
their eyes gelling with light,
their tails lifted high,
necks outstretched,
seeking something other
than what we could give them.
Absorbed, intent,
they faced danger bravely,
as though they knew
a surplus of deer
brings guns.
And although they seemed
at one with the winter grass,
brown oaks, green hemlock,
they carried the weight of death
with their beauty.

TO MY MOTHER

Last year
at this time
you fractured your back
again
and I brought you tea,
helped fix dinner,
went shopping,
put you to bed.

You have abandoned
so many gardens
and they grow wild.
A lone crocus
blooms in the front yard—
the rest of it hungry weed.

I wonder how many
springs we will still
see together,
the roses in
the back undaunted
and gulping
light, this summer
as last summer,
the bruised wisteria
still clutching the base of the home.

SLEEP

Of all
things
in the world
I would like to be granted rest.
Having been wakeful for nights
I want to sleep
oblivious
of everything,
even the single
deaf tree
left from winter
as it beckons.

YOUR HAND

Inert, inured, your hand lay cold on mine.
I still recall when we met, the little time
it took me to lift myself from sleep,
the morning white like a hundred sheep

walking. Yet you weren't cold
in those days. We grow old
so slowly, and we begin to change
before we recognize how the changes impinge.

Nearing you every day then veering away,
I can still see your pale eyes facing me
telling me, I want a love
that does not go on forever but awhile—like a glove

that frays and we tear it off and then desist.
Still, we cannot stop, but must persist.

DO THE DEAD?

Do the dead stop and rest,
or do they continue?
I once saw their world,
the unchanging chasms of red
like whorls of evening clouds,
sea-green and bottle greens.
A voice spoke to me
loud and soft,
with a sound
like a fly beating its wings
against paper.

Do the dead retire to living rooms
where they drink tea and coffee?
Do they chat with
their neighbors about unruly
sunsets and the summer weather?
Undo the rope
laces on their shoes,
pause to think of
what happened when they were alive?

Does their living flash
back to them
like something they cannot reach
a world behind a window
with birds flapping by
whose nests were disturbed?
Do they regret it?
Do they clutch at it

the way I clutch at a few
stars in a cloudy night-sky?

Do the angels
remain aloof
their faces invisible
never beheld
curtained,
swallowing their laughter
hiccups pouring out like medicine?

MY HANDS

hold nothing. water
pouring to the dark earth
pushed by the wheels of cars and bicycles,
gulls with their winding paths
tulip and May flowers in the garden.
My hands hold nothing
the night sky
clutching a few stars.
You were here once
and there is a dead space you left.
And I have said
nothing and known nothing
just as the tree says nothing
and knows nothing
but feels the wind
move about
through leaves, branches.

Rain

Count rain on my fingers?
It is too fine,
like each column of pain—
my hands hold it gingerly,
till it runs through them.

A swan
ruffling her feathers
after dunking.

Her neck arched
orange bill shining.

SICKNESS

Mornings sick lying in bed
the dawn comes with flutes—
warbler, catbird, chickadee,
pulling in the spring light.

I have been dreaming about
a man in black clothes, chasing
me through a labyrinth.
The rooms full of windows get
smaller and smaller. I can't
escape.

I want to fight him with my fists.
Why can't death cover me like my own breath,
make a single sound like the sea
wave after wave
full of memory,
the fish opening their mouths on the crest?

ODE TO THE SEA
after Neruda

rivers mouth you.
kiss you with silver
fish joining.

Whatever is unknown—
that you are.
Fishermen, boats rocking,
dawn smearing red paint over blue,
the evening like a lost cat meowing
for water and food.

I heave myself up against you,
swim.
And you are like a crow cawing
its hidden words
on branches, sky.

THE SEAL

A seal rests
on our beach, his flippers
shining, bringing with him
the taste of fish and spawn.

Every morning I get up
to greet him with my
father. Bald, seventyish,
he does nothing
but golf
and watch television.

As a young man
he didn't have spite,
pointing out to me how to
slice into the ball,
shoot straight down
the fairway and to putt.

Now we don't speak.
He sits cornered in the
other room by the
television,
golf on his mind,
his blunt words
only for the sportscasters.

Now we are going to see the seal—
not knowing if he
is sick, or

taking a vacation
from the icy north.

I hold my breath
each time I see him,
But my father wants
to swim with him,
and they seem to
dance together
in my mind,
the one wild, wielding
his weight,
free of a past,
the other tied down
by doings I cannot undo.

THE LAKE AND MY CHILDHOOD

What set off the fire
over the lake at night?
I can still see the beavers' tails
flapping
the fish born there sliming
through water to drink air.
The cottages at the lakefront are
incandescent with their electric light,
and I in my shadow house
where there is so much solitude,
a cuff around my wrist.

In the mornings at the lake
I see the haze
of bees around bushes,
hear tiny songs of birds,
but I am like a tree
that thinks thoughts
none can hear.
The tree does not lift its leaves
as it drinks water from the dark earth it clutches,
yet my thoughts edge
to the wind,
soil, leaves, sky.

II.

The Street
Where I Was
a Child

JOURNEY

On the train
the strangers' faces
look older than the faces
I saw as a child.
The car is covered with a fall of ashes,
and as they leave, night bends over the passengers.

I am measuring how much distance
I have come, to get to
the largeness of this place,
nearly halfway
from where I started,
only to be surprised by the emptiness
of this night, and all nights,
and the ten lumps of light in the station-street
that shed haloes in the air.
I see how my whole life follows me,
others' lives,
everything we share
and everything we suffer and cannot share,
present, clear in my mind,
when I have turned.

THE BEGGAR AND HIS DOG

He came out of the coffee shop
with the round hamburger
with which he taught his dog to beg.

His eyes glowed, bright and blank
as Christmas ornaments.
He had a piece of fabric for a tie,
and a torn old black suit.

Like a magician's suit,
or an actor's,
he was more dressed than usual.
His reels and swerves were bows,
his dog was a performer.

While the dog begged
he nodded smiles,
his skin loose,
his eyes wobbling.

It was Sunday.
In his black suit,
with no money, but still a dog,
he was out to show off his family.

THE MOOSE

The day the moose
broke the silence
of the wood
where we had walked all day,
I was twelve,
stood next to my father,
his eyebrows thick and soft,
face strange and cold.

Crows drifted in
and out of the trees.
The mountains ran humpbacked.
When we left the tent,
he pointed out the sky, fields,
and mosquitoes. I looked away
down the path where moths fluttered,
and would not answer him.

Then the moose swung,
its dark back lifted
against the cold sky,
leaves and brittle twigs trembling—
our fingers stationed so closely together.
It did not see us,
went past the path,
its whole weight
forward,
eastward.

THE STREET WHERE I WAS A CHILD

Trains cross it like small ponies,
traveling west, their dark hooves
beating, their backs weighted with
cargo, as if in the west
wealth was commonplace.

The trees sag with the wisdom
of having stayed in the same place
a lifetime.

A man comes out of a green door
across from mine
to pluck roses.
His eyes are shining.
Is there some terror in them,
as he stoops over
the soft, thorny plants?

I want to ask him what it will be like
to go on living
for a hundred years.
His hands are light and small
fingers clumped,
eyes blue.

He brings the flowers to his wife,
slips beneath the shade trees
to sit and read.
I am five years old.
The sun shines hard as a baseball.

THE WALK TO THE HARBOR

It was still early when we walked
to the harbor. The black water
was bitten by new snow.   The pipes
in the houses gushed from the melting,
and slush whispered under the cars.
We were lost in life as orphans
that morning we stopped to see the daffodils,
flowers, buds, leaves
just opening with a brightness
like the brightness that comes from drawing near the future.

I wonder where all those futures are—
we talked of many that day, but never lived one.
In this sparse place they are a brightness
just out of reach, like the flowers we saw,
yellow against concrete,
then flattened, dried, altered
two or three weeks later on.
But the spring lapped us up then
and we forgot ourselves,
as I want to forget myself now,
walking out under a hard sky,
my thoughts bent toward winter,
I think of the past and rain starts
and ticks around me like time.

DRY LEAVES

One afternoon last September
after the rain stopped,
and mist rose
there was a feeling
of leaves which were burning,
as they were burnt
in rusted wire cans
up and down my avenue
years ago.
On warm days the old men wore undershirts
and sat out
in lounge chairs,
watched,
and smoked cigars.
It was a mixture of bright and dark,
a chiaroscuro
as they caught on fire.

AUGUST

The leaves lift up. There are blossoms,
a small quiet dog,
my brother and mother
huddled at a wooden vacation table
playing cards.

My father sits opposite,
motionless,
except that he slaps
the mosquitoes with his pale hands.

He bends his head, talks suddenly
about Tom Sawyer whitewashing a fence,
how once, years ago, in rural
Indiana, he painted the small,
lopsided houses for
fifty cents an hour
at age seventeen,
left to come east,
and never returned.

Night falls. We walk out
separately. The moon papers
everything so clearly,
the clumped trees, lake,
the pale hair on his hands.

EVENING WITH MY FATHER

Last Tuesday I played tennis with him.
We slapped balls easily.
His voice sounded friendly,
as if we had done more
than face each other
strangers across newspapers,
and I had asked more of him,
than questions about spaghetti sauces
and loans.

We were not quite friends that night,
but I thought of the blue room,
where I was six or seven
and my father told me stories
of salmon caught in California rivers,
and bear fur left on trees in the Indiana town
where he grew up.
As he talked,
the small darkness in the room's corner
would begin lifting,
thick then with thieves and wild-eyed dancers
as it is thick now with unknowns.

FIVE LEAVES

Soon I will need all the silence
of this morning to shield me:
snow falling through emptiness,
the last five leaves on a tree, abrupt in the sky,
like five flat hands, gathering whiteness.
I am growing very patient inside,
and I am going far
over some shaking emptiness,
till I can come back,
needing this silent morning.

THE DEER

Yesterday the deer came
to the window,
her head lifted, fearless
and beautiful even to the corners
of her eyes.
All afternoon she balanced easily,
waited through the twilight
still, proud.
I thought of children
who walk for years
through streets they do not know,
their heads upright,
seeking.
And although I walk heavily to the window,
and see little in the world outside,
I know this will not always be so,
as it is not so
for this deer,
as she moves,
fragile, unafraid
of what she loves.

RAIN

That summer the rain
touched the pavement like wounded fingers.
The sky fell down at night,
and in the mornings
sadness rose up from the ground.
Men and women in the shops
and the concession stands
near the railroads
were exhausted.
More people were traveling
to some new destination,
with only a single, slung bag,
alone.

I went to a tinsel diner
that sold creampuffs and jelly donuts.
A beggar who had recently lost his only friend,
roamed in and out the door
looking for him with large eyes,
and called everyone by his name.

A man was there from Seattle,
who mentioned there was a table
he liked to sit at which overlooked
an open field. Flowers grew in pairs
there. The birds found food.
He said he felt peace there, without effort,
when he was alone. I told him of friends
I had known in two cities.
Their coming and going had been easy.
Nothing had hurt as it should have.
It had been easy as breathing air.

THE SUMMER HOUSE

The summer house
leans, as if terrified
by us, a little to
one side. My father
stoops through
the airy wooden doorway,
wanders slowly, quietly,
and eyes me as if he
meant to be honest,
but could not.

I am standing,
eating a vanilla ice cream cone.
Mosquitoes swarm.
There is a thought
in my mind,
like a lump in my
throat, a bump
on a log,
that my hand goes over
and over again.

My father ventures
out into the afternoon
which is heartless
as the beginning
of the world.

Geese honk
with a sound thin as paper,

then melt toward the horizon.

There is a space
my father leaves
behind him, wide
as the needle
the camel couldn't walk through
or the rich man.

In the ephemeral light
of the July afternoon
we sit over supper.
We hesitate,
speak our thoughts.

GULLS

In that moment when the fires of the stars die
before the next fire comes,
the gulls rise,
filling the empty sky like numberless dreams,
pale and careless, floating on the air.

And I think how hard it has been sometimes,
to say a word
when I know I will hear it echo
from one galaxy to the next,
and even to stoop, lift someone
softly out of pain,
takes patience,
and a heart like stone to bear
the incompleteness of that action.

Their wings hang like hands,
and their motions reassure me.
Peace
before the light.

THERE IS NO CHILDHOOD NOW

The streets stretch large and dark
and the birds learn to lean
on the new, raw snow.
Everyone I know,
misses things that happened years ago,
They listen to the air by the sea
that shakes the shutters and doors,
howls, like someone wronged.

And I wonder why I cannot return
to the summer
when my brother and I
rowed the boat to the green, shining fish,
dropped down
yellow flies each evening,
month after month, sun or rain,
and played with toy Indians
posed on a shelf
we pretended was a mountain.

Yet now there are only people
 who glide into my life
and do not seem to leave. I hear their
footsteps, but remember
how mother was once
light and gentle as a sparrow,
and I grow preoccupied
with a blue, round room,
and think, in the sea
the dolphins are still diving
as we once did, in the waves.

WHOSE CRIES ARE NOT MUSIC

I come down to the dark, torn pond
to hear the geese
whose cries are not music, but
catch in my ears:
the cry of wild birds
who can make only one sound
and put into that sound
wing-beat, empty marshes,
clouds and their quests
for home.

They have traveled miles,
are far from earth
when I hear them,
but I think of a child
who has no words
and will cry without stopping.
as if everything
must begin in pain.

I can spend my whole life
healing it,
but find in the end
that love itself contains pain
though I do not give up feeling it,
as today I do not give up
hearing these geese
whose cries are constant,
and I pause
as their shrillness softens
and the light fades
and the night comes with silence.

THIS SILENCE

It is always the same silence I come to,
the silence of snow curving over a roof,
filling air, trees, wires, shutters.
And you know you will have to keep
stretching this silence you find yourself in,
till it is large enough
to put both your hands through it,
and someone else's hands,
clap them together
till they ring like an opening door.

III.
For Mary

ON WRITING POETRY

I.

The August evening light falls over us.
Words scatter between us,
They seem to come from beyond the two purple hills,
tell of your suffering,
the early death
doctors predict for you.
In the yard
a sparrow is separating its wings,
In another country
a soldier uses
his only arm to drink water.

II.

Droplets of rain start,
wet on my face.
I know you and
the speech that patters between us.
I feel the meanings
without yet knowing them.

WINTER

The silence of the snow
this winter
was like two hands praying.

And what do they pray for,
the hands and silent pots draped
with the dishtowel to dry?

After your death
I sat in the dark room
and watched the single fluorescent light
glint on my teacup..

What is the meaning of being alive?
Is it the world coming close
to ending,—
is it two hands
clasped, meeting?
After the whiteness—
the new green shoots rising?

CLOUD

Fuzzy, it hangs
between the two segments
of blue the way
you hung your left hand
over the white chair
when I was in the room.

How distinct each memory is.
We raked leaves
through October
around the chrysanthemums
and beds of bulbs.
The clouds lay flat then—
slabs of white stone.

I can still hear your
voice punctuated by
the scraping of the rakes,
getting at the meanings
without wholly being able
to say them.

In your absence,
the clouds are puffy
as if a multitude of tragedies
had gotten inside them
swelling them
like the undersides of eyes.

OTHER VOICES

I know now
The dead talk to us.

And I wonder
Why the stones have been here so long,
And words seem to fall
Into water to be washed again
Or turn into stories.

It is the kind of November day
I can walk for miles in,
See the sky as a vista
Of the entire universe.
Cloud layers upon cloud,
Like in Mesa cliff dwellers' houses,
As if space could go on forever.

Does it go on forever?
Or does it stop abruptly
Like a blank unnamed wall.

"Why should life stop?"
You seemed to say
One day when we were walking
Through this park
The leaves auburn, red, yellow.
Yet you propped your head up
On pillows two years later
And wheezed with every sentence.

Still those words turn into stories
And I grasp this sky
Without being able to understand
Why I am standing beneath it,
Still talking to the dead.

EMISSARIES

I.

Coming at dawn, the rabbits
seem emissaries from a better,
spiritual realm, their faces round
and kind, their forms
filtered in the half-light.

I wonder if the dead can hear us?
Does your spirit, Mary, find the old places—
dead leaves clumped in a pile
where the trail forked,
the crows with their voices flailing
and muscled sound, warning the other
birds of our approach.
We loved these trees,
the churning winds.
We waited in the dusk
for the summer evening,
the darkness turning in
to sleep over the woods.

II.

If I do not know
What love is,
I can wait out the darkness
Till morning comes,
The light claps its hands
And shines.

Then the fish tremble
Through the summer pond,
Their eyes clear, bodies gleaming
Green.

You are not here, Mary,
But I find you
In the sun singing
In the sky—
In so much blue.
The clouds speak to the dead,
And you watch over me,
all afternoon,
where shadows do not yet cluster
in the garden,
nor in my waiting mind.

EYES FIERCE AS A BLUEFISH

It's been four years—
you seem caged
on the other side of death
and I cannot reach you.
What absorbs the hills?
Sunlight and shadow.
I think we will always
be in half-dark now.
I try calling out to you
but you—
with eyes fierce
as a bluefish's
smooth hands aligned
on your lap—
don't say a word.

WHEN THE ROADS CRY OUT

When that day
No longer comes,
When the roads cry out
Because of their endlessness,
And the frozen rivers
Crackle as they break
With the new spring,
And I am no longer
Able to lift myself
Out of despair
Because you were once all around,
Your face
Surrounding me,
Your voice
Speaking only of the future—
Then I will reflect
On seas with current
Flowing north,
Ice and glaciers,
Freezing and uninhabitable.

STARS

These nights I feel empty,
though my hands retain the strength
they had when I knew you.

Someday the polluted skies
will conceal the stars,
Ursa Major, Pleiades, the archer whom
the gods destroyed because he wanted to kill all the animals,
and his taut bow lost at sea.
Now it seems that everything I love
must disappear;
bright trout playing in light
in a darkening stream.

DREAM

If the dream persists, the one
Where you are standing
Uttering nothing and
I am trying to take your photo,
We might stand like that
For all eternity,
Me praising your corn-colored hair
The straightness of your spine
Your eyes quivering in the light.
Where is God
But in a dream where
The light between us, always yellow,
Yields like sunlight
Never fading into oblivion,
Even after you open your mouth,
I am done with the photograph and
Speech begins.

AFTER YOUR DEATH

Your death
seems to pray though this snow,
each white petal
bitter because it is still winter,
and you died in winter,
on Valentine's Day.

Soon I will have to make
tea from the plastic pot,
the steam erupting
out makes everything shine,
the forks, kitchen table, plates
nicked pine of the table.

What is the meaning of the encounter?
Two hands meet,
intersect.
These cold days we know we are still alive.

THE POEM

If I go into the wood,
in February snow
and it is barren,
empty white
against thick tree trunks,
then I have found nothing.
But if a deer waits there,
all movement,
eyes full of shine,
back coated with cold
and winter sunlight,
then I am allowed to return to the fields
I have lost in my mind,
first red ranch house I lived in,
lanky earth pushed
by wind, grass undulating,
the evening full of deer.

DREAMS

These dreams have been here a long time.
The wind has many hands.
In a paddock a red horse
nuzzles his nose against a fence.
I feel the color of the bright winter day.
Everything the birds seek
can be found.

LEAVE MY HOUSE

I want to leave my house—
Turn to the home I grew up in,
The white hollow rooms,
The straight chairs,
Their backs breathing.
The scowl
Gone from my father's face,
His hands burrowing
For use, touching
Wood, metal.
No one has died,
No one ill,
No one lost.

MORE THAN THE TIME WE NEEDED

I startled the stones
And they made a crying sound
From where I stand
You are years away
At sea,
On a lime-colored beach
The waves imprint on.
In my dreams,
You write me,
But someone wakes me
Before I am finished
Reading your letter.
I balk at the sound
Of that other voice,
Chalky and indistinct,
Pulling me from sleep,
And shun the objects in the room,
Dresser, desk,
Comb and brush,
Mirror.
The stones are oozing
From the mountain river-bed,
Making a sound like a forest crying,
So different from us,
Where we once stood together,
With what seemed
More than the time we needed
Talking.

THE SEA

Like a sponge takes in
Sunlight.   Yellow and red
Fish use its water.
Lapping up around a single island,
How like a bright tongue are its waves.

IV.

ST. PAUL STREET

DEPARTURES

How empty the room,
bright.
Its shapes soft,
as if we had both played there
as children, and
I had advanced my toy soldiers
over the kitchen table
which was a smooth ledge,
and planned a defense
you could not break through.
But the salt and pepper shakers
were strange and downcast.
Two large bags of trash,
two chairs stood speechless
over the kitchen floor.

It was my doggedness
that kept me going then,
walking through the spring,
past the flowers in pots in the garden,
and the people with their houses
in their cars,
traveling westward
or south,
early in the morning
desperate for work.

I went west too,
with a rusted iron in my back seat,
bags of clothing,

and the windows rolled down to let in
the open arms of the warm air.

People passed by,
cities, trees.
It kept getting brighter and warmer.
I went on, not looking back,
and the world curved around me
quietly, carelessly,
and told me its story.

ST. PAUL STREET

So many of us who came
to this red row house on St. Paul Street
lay in bed at night
looking out the window at the stars.
We ached with the darkness,
wanting all we could not have.
Leaving home and family,
we came here to recover
from depression, mixed up lives.
One sultry afternoon
I told you how lucky you were.
You whispered to me,
"I have a boyfriend, but I'm not lucky."

Yet we envied you.
None of us believed
you would throw yourself off the five-story house.

The next day three gulls disappeared
behind the building
returned, curving in the air.
The sentences I squeezed out were hollow.
The words weighed on each other.
Every word ached.
I could not grasp my sorrow.
Words fell down
like houses of cards,
one unleashing pain into the next.

CANADA GEESE

Sixty
rested on the incline
of the far field,
immobile, blending
in with the undergrowth
and thin snow.
I had forgotten,
if I had followed the north trail
that led back to my home
or had made some wrong turn
into the center of the park.
Only the geese
stopped there,
resting
in rows,
hungry and bitterly cold.
They made jittery motions,
flapped wings
stood up in the air,
stretched their long necks,
exposed their pale under-wings,
flew skywards,
then bore east.
They made a sound as sad
as a child's cries.
The white hill was empty,
narrow, brown spaces left
where the thinnest layer of snow
had melted from the heat of their heavy bodies.

THE CITY

I do not know where my joy
came from in that city—
from the rats
idling in the daylight
their faces half-intelligent and crude?
From the birds slanting to the trees in the park
in the air that seemed to beg for silence,
its harmony formed by
cars, trucks slamming?
Or from the homeless people,
strangers, some of them,
from distant cities.
who spent their day with bottles,
and stretched to sleep
with half-open eyes
on benches at mid afternoon?
Or from the spring,
the trees with red half-leaves,
the streets thick with people,
from remembering my childhood,
as I could then?
Or from midnight and the resting air?
The cars were gone,
stranger called to stranger
up and down the avenue
as if they were friends.

THIS CAT

This cat was a stray,
neglected, given up on,
roaming my street
in hopes for a morsel
some stranger threw away,
outdoors in snow, rain,
feeling the singe of the summer sun.
I tried to take her in,
gave her food, water
a home,
but she roamed with her tail
turned toward me
down another street,
preferring to be wild.

I remember
wandering rainy roads,
gone for days,
liking that better
than sitting at supper,
with food on the table,
a knife and fork nearby.
It was as if
I knew domesticity
but preferred wildness.
rain needling my face,
the thick bite of winter snow.

YOU WANDERED

That summer you wandered
long, eyes wide.
arms flapping at your side,
hands empty,
into streets where men idled
and sang like broken guitars
where wind beat empty paper
and oozy water wrinkled
in the harbor
under boats humming by.
Your thoughts slid
between the sounds,
and you lost your money to strangers—
one a beggar, another an artist
in a green coat
selling paintings in the park
for a hundred dollars.
Poor, all his hungers had made him sharp,
as all your hungers had weakened you:
your arms, legs, head
hung from you—
lost, unwanted belongings,
the tails of a child's kite,
flopping at the air.
In fall you rested, closed
the shades in the house halfway on the light.
told me of everyone you had lost
in your life—John, who was ill
and lived in Virginia, David
who was wild and left you and came back

and left you for someone else.
A stillness hung over you,
your arms glided back
from coffee to cigarette,
regular as music, still and bare.
You smiled like a sparrow, shyly,
with only a little fear—
telling me your life was clear
in your mind now,
and everything that had come before was past.
Today a hard rain
shivers on the streets,
leaks off the roofs,
swirls in the gutters,
and everything shares
the noise of falling,
and the city blurs almost
to one single thought:
a neon rain,
hard as my hands.
I turn off the lights
and ignition of my car,
get out.
go down the gray streets
to where you are standing,
your face lined by thirty-seven years
although in your eyes
a speck of joy comes through.
You are scuffing the pavement,
rain-drenched, in second-hand shoes.

SPRING IN THE CITY

The white blossoms feathered the edges of the streets.
The bellies of the new leaves
were bloodshot
and we lay awake three nights
on the grass in the dark park,
the spring sharp in our mouths
like a knife,
while around us,
all the roads leaped,
the gray gulls
rocked up close, mewed
at the distant sky
When you left me.
I sat still for days,
watched a friend's face change,
smile, ease, then stop smiling,
a beggar drink
and a sparrow
from the same stream.
There was no silence
in my mind.
My thoughts ticked accurate and dull
as a clock,
and time lapsed
like a broken horn
with only a little music left,
bleating.

TO MARGARET

When I heard that news
I walked for hours,
remembered how we settled five years ago
in that red row house,
hunched over meals,
slipped out in the sloppy rain,
after cigarettes, drinks, men.
I remember
your smile, that some days
believed in itself completely,
your dark hair and eyes like mine,
Mondays in the pizza parlor
called Never on Sunday,
Tuesdays in the dark local bar.
Up and down
the New Jersey Turnpike
I thought of you—
yet we were never close friends,
and in those days
I could never like
my own resemblance.

For years we were roommates,
yet only rarely looked up
at the moon, blinked
at the sun, only rarely
remembered what it is
that people do when they know
that they, too, can feel.
But the railings on these buildings

are iron and cold.
The rain rings
like tambourines in my ears.

In summer
the dust falls
speck by speck,
and I know
we were uprooted,
went everywhere hard,
yet never strong.
uncertain
like flowers that swung
in a wind too full of its own longings
to hold us—
living and striving
in this gray city called Baltimore,
the city where you died
on a winter day.
You could not feel
that we loved you,
as we did,
yet only as other travelers can,
never quite at ease
in these loud streets, never singing.

JOHN

I wonder where I met you first John,
on the stoop in front of my house
that felt like sand?
Your face was shining,
as you told me you had become happy.
You found friends,
something you never had before.
When you were younger,
you closed your bedroom door to cry
and nothing cried with you.

In school you left the busy halls
for empty bathrooms,
spoke to no one—no one spoke to you.
and when you went home,
the brown drab fields said nothing to you.

Now your face shines,
but only as fireflies
which light up the night
that surrounds them
for a moment.
I know inside you feel darkness,
and I wish I could help you lift it,
as I try to lift my own, slowly,
puzzling over memories
clear and strange
as my own name.

AFTER FIVE YEARS
(for James)

I seem to meet you again
after five years,
in the middle of September,
in a place where I can only hear
geese honk out of icy,
fragments of throats.

When you died
the morning was like
a thick, gray horse.

I went alone in a train
which wound from New York to Ohio,
where I was born,
through states I did not know,
then traveled slowly through a lush, wet, green Louisiana
where you grew up.

Something lifted me over the space
which bridged the train and the world of the dead.
The dead were colored purple and green.
They floated like clouds
in the changing air.
There was only a single voice talking,
with a sound like a faucet dripping,
or thin rain.

I would like to wish
you back to life.

You were here
five years ago in summer.
We talked at a table outdoors.
but the distance between us
grew hard to encompass,
like the stone table between us.

You died
when I was away,
restless, at a lake
under an even-shining sun, rowing.
Air separates the clouds.
The geese unhinge the muscles of the sky.
The air is changed from their honking.
I replace you with myself,
breathing in this red, dazed day,
feeling the hours wear thin,
as they repeat themselves,
and erode
and drive hard into whatever
is in this world.

THERE IS NO STILLNESS

There is no stillness
in the room we left empty.
The broken kettle
does not sputter like an engine,
and Michael
who one day wore drag
the next
left for Kentucky
on a job
checking air conditioners
with a waitress
he'd picked up
the night before
to marry is gone.
John,
who smiled over coffee
tore napkins with his fingers
while he told us
he'd found
what he needed most
and never had—
friends—
last May 15
stopped wanting to live.
And you and I, Billy
have stopped praying to the same god
we prayed to that last day
we were together
on the curved stone bench
by the fountain

whose idle water
mixed up streetlights
and the moon.
You said then
you once made
a vow to be silent
till the world changed
and only broke it,
when you came up with a better idea.

I am alone now,
across from me
on the trees
the cones are still,
hard,
a slight wind stirs them,
they slide,
rock,
but do not open,
are always tight
like the fists of children
who hold themselves to themselves.
Not long ago
I went on a train trip
to a new city.
In the window
lights and
stranger's faces
passed by.

They were older
than the faces

I remember
seeing as a child;
their bodies
still
stone-like
tired,
as if they had been awake
for hours,
waiting.

Outside today
loud crow-chatter.
I name the names of friends
but do not find them
and I have stopped praying
to them in my mind.

MILK CRATES

They are picking up the milk crates
in this store, whose owners I know,
placing them in rows
in the grey backroom
to sleep, neatly,
with empty potato sacks
a few green-printed boxes,
things too well made to be useless,
though they can't find uses for them right away.
On a corner on Broadway
I found him, that week in November,
my friend from a religious retreat,
sitting on a milk-crate,
under a ledge which just kept out the rising rain.
He talked to me with eyes rolled back,
his hands in the pockets of a green coat I remembered,
as he told me,
it was a way of life he'd chosen
and the raining streets,
people who passed quickly
were more real to him
than what he'd had
six months ago, in March,
sitting on a lawn and talking
about God and the meaning of dreams.

In the supermarket
I measured the time it took them,

to unpack the black and brown potatoes from the sacks,
the pale tomatoes and winter apples,
the milk from crates,
throwing out the loose paper
and saving the rest for strange uses, like my friend's.

THE HAWK

Hawk landed a few feet
From me. Three feet tall.
Wings closed. I am in danger
But don't move. This is not
An apparition of a hawk,
But a hawk.

She came from the woods
To the north.
I am often quiet
As I walk through them,
And chipmunks crisscross the path,
The lone deer makes herself
Visible to me,
The undergrowth tears my shoes.

I don't want to leave the woods
For the row house in the city
Where you died,
Deep in depression,
Throwing yourself off
The five story building,
And everyone around you
Unable to explain.
Yet we went out to breakfast,
Went to discos in the evenings,
Took walks

I am afraid someday
I will wake

Fearful and speechless,
The azalea blooming red
And remember that house,
Framed only by concrete
All the people I knew there moved away or gone.

UNDER A MORNING THAT HAS
NO BLOSSOMS

I fear sometimes
I may wake up alone,
under a morning that has no blossoms,
and walk again over the corpses of things—
gulls disappearing over a curved shore,
sudden, swift, sure.
a room with stiff chairs that was home
for a year, the people coming and going, gone.

The sea seems to toss up its fears to the sky
till morning.
I sift, age:
a morning of differences,
a memory of turning in time.

V.

AFTER DEATH

THIS IS THE FINAL DAY OF YEARS OF SWEETNESS
(Petrarch)

She came north every summer
Nested in the ilex,
Sat on the metal pole
That marks the oil burner tank
In our yard,
And wanted to do nothing but sing.

My mother remembers waking to the
Plain bird's song early in the spring mornings—
As if happiness could begin at sunrise,
Last till evening,
And days could be spent in praise.

When I discovered the catbird's rumpled body,
A hand's span of grey feathers left
Every other part of her disappeared,
She seemed to have no words for me.

I wonder still why she cannot
Return south this year with her mate
Bring up fledglings,
Sit in the sun and praise
As if praising were everything,
Dying and living nothing.

Jonah, trapped in the belly of the whale,
Surrounded by darkness and shining skin,
Spoke to god and he was released.
Yet she cannot be released from this death,
Or speak to us anymore.

FOUR DEER

Today I walked past Mrs. Clay's
And her daughter Megan's house,
Down the block to the strangers' wooded yard,
Where once four deer stood.

I waited for their stillness
And their shadows, their heads
Bent, looking, as if curious
About all they saw.

Last summer Megan rested,
Legs crossed, hair
Curly, sitting on the beach
Talking to a group of
Her mother's friends, their backs
To the sun. Her
Mother always said hello to me
Before getting in the water.

Megan and I went swimming at different times,
Keeping up with the tides.
We nodded
As we both sat
Beside the older women, listening.

When I heard she got cancer
Everything seemed to
Tremble.
The deer
Appearing in the woods again

Stared at me as I
Walked by.

In that stare an eternity seemed to sit,
Death and heaven
And the stillness of God.

DANCE

I rolled out my fingers
to touch the blossoming
azalea this spring,
as you lifted your arms
to be in harmony
with music.
We each excelled at what we did,
but neither was equal
to dying, the soul compressed,
dried, flattened,
the hands extended
as if still reaching to touch
the dream that is no longer there,
and the dream that is coming.

IN DYING

I return to the piebald hills
Where only birds sing
Praise, and I cannot pretend
To have forgotten
Your sputtering dance,
Your dark dipping eyes.
Don't I always turn back
To you when I am ill
Or alone,
Like a dancer remembering
The dance?
The husk comes away from the seed.
Don't we in dying
Reveal who we are?

LINDA IS PUBLISHED IN NUMEROUS
magazines, most recently Canary: a Journal of
the Environmental Crisis, OCHO, Oranges
and Sardines and Agenda. She has published 5
chapbooks and won a chapbook contest at Kritya
in India. She graduated with honors from Johns
Hopkins University where she was an English
major. She has a MA in English with an emphasis
on creative writing from Stony Brook. She is former
assistant poetry editor at womenwriters.net, and was
shortlisted for the Cinnamon Press Prize in poetry.

ABOUT THE LUMMOX PRESS

LUMMOX PRESS was created in 1994 by RD Armstrong. It began as a self-publishing/DIY imprint for poetry by RD. Several chapbooks were published and in late 1995 it began publishing the Lummox Journal, a monthly small/underground press lit-arts mag. Available primarily by subscription, the LJ continued its exploration of the "creative process" until its demise as a print mag in 2006. It was hailed as one of the best monthlies in the small press.

In 1998, Lummox began publishing the Little Red Book series, and continues to do so today. To date there are some 59 titles in the series (as of 2010) and a collection of poems from the first decade of the series has been published under the title, The Long Way Home (2009); it's a great way to explore the series.

Together with Chris Yeseta (Layout and Art Direction since 1997), RD continues to publish books that are both striking in their looks as well as their content...you'd think he was aping Black Sparrow, but he is merely trying to produce the best books he can for his clients, the poets, and their customers, you, the readers.

The following books are available directly from the Lummox Press via its website: www.lummoxpress.com or at Lummox, c/o PO Box 5301, San Pedro, CA 90733. There are also E-Book (PDF) versions of most titles available. Most of these titles are available through other book sellers online, as well.

The Wren Notebook by Rick Smith (2000)
Last Call: The Legacy of Charles Bukowski
    edited by RD Armstrong (2004)
On/Off the Beaten Path by RD Armstrong (2008)

Fire and Rain–Selected Poems 1993-2007 *Volumes 1 & 2*
  by RD Armstrong (2008)
El Pagano and Other Twisted Tales by RD Armstrong
  (short stories–2008)
New and Selected Poems by John Yamrus (2009)
The Riddle of the Wooden Gun by Todd Moore (2009)
Sea Trails by Pris Campbell (2009)
Down This Crooked Road–Modern Poetry from the Road
  Less Traveled edited by RD Armstrong and William
  Taylor, Jr. (2009)
The Long Way Home edited by RD Armstrong (2009)
Drive By by John Bennett (2010)
Modest Aspirations by Gerald Locklin & Beth Wilson (2010)
Steel Valley by Michael Adams (2010)
Hard Landing by Rick Smith (2010)
A Love Letter to Darwin by Jane Crown (2010)
E/OR–Living Amongst the Mangled by RD Armstrong (2010)

www.ingramcontent.com/pod-product-compliance
Lightning Source LLC
Chambersburg PA
CBHW020920090426
42736CB00008B/723